REFLECTIONS OF THE LAW IN LITERATURE

Reflections of the Law
in Literature

by

F. LYMAN WINDOLPH

PHILADELPHIA
UNIVERSITY OF PENNSYLVANIA PRESS

Library of Congress Catalogue Card Number 56–9738

Published in Great Britain, India, and Pakistan
by Geoffrey Cumberlege: Oxford University Press,
London, Bombay, and Karachi

PRINTED IN THE UNITED STATES OF AMERICA
BY AMERICAN BOOK-STRATFORD PRESS, INC., NEW YORK

These lectures were delivered at Franklin and Marshall College on March 24 and 25, 1955, through the North Foundation, established by a bequest of Hugh M. North, Jr., to provide for annual lectures on law or allied subjects.

Contents

REFLECTIONS OF THE LAW IN LITERATURE

Trollope and the Law

THE North bequest provides for lectures on "the law or allied subjects." A list of the titles selected by earlier lecturers suggests a wide range of inquiry. You will remember what Louis XIV said after listening to a sermon by a famous preacher: "If he had talked a little about God, he would have talked a little about everything." I am not willing to run the risk of so devastating a criticism. After a fashion, at least, we are going to stick to our knitting. This morning I am going to speak about "Trollope and the Law," this evening about "Shakespeare and the Law," and tomorrow evening about "Browning and the Law." In short, no matter what judgment you may pass on the lectures themselves, I propose to make it impossible for you or anyone to paraphrase King Louis by saying that if I had talked a little about the law, I would have talked a little about everything.

I have mentioned Trollope, and the man to whom I am referring is, of course, Anthony Trollope, the English novelist of the nineteenth century. I must record myself at the outset as included in the steadily growing number of his admirers. It seems like a happy mixture of boldness and prudence for a man to offer to make bets which, in the nature of the case, he can neither win nor lose in the course of his lifetime. In that spirit I offer to bet that if our civilization persists—a condition which I find myself unable to take for granted—the novels of Trollope will be read and enjoyed longer than those of either Dickens or Thackeray. Be that as it may, and whether I have any takers or not, I think I need tell you nothing about Trollope beyond calling attention to the fact that in half a dozen of his novels he dealt more or less at length, and with varying degrees of accuracy and sympathy, with lawyers and legal problems. I must confine myself this morning to a single one of these novels—*Phineas Redux,* which is the sequel to an earlier story called *Phineas Finn.*

Phineas Finn, who is the hero of both stories, was the only son of Dr. Malachi Finn of Killaloe, West Ireland. His father was a successful physician who had, however, a costly family of five (as yet) unmarried daughters and the son whom he proposed to educate for the bar. Phineas attended Trinity College in Dublin, where he joined a debating society in which he achieved some distinction, and where no doubt was born the secret ambition to become a member of the English Parliament. When he finished college at the age of twenty-two he persuaded his father to let him read for the bar in London. If, in the ensuing three years, he did not show any special zeal or aptitude for his intended profession, he at least furthered his secret ambition by becoming a member of the leading Whig Club—the Reform Club —and by making a number of politically influential friends. He was called to the bar just when the Tory government of the day had been defeated, Parliament was to be dissolved and elections were to follow. When, therefore, one of his friends of the Reform Club, Barrington Erle by name, urged him to stand for a seat in Parliament for the Irish borough of Loughshane, Phineas was strongly tempted. There was much to be said against taking this step. At that time members of Parliament received no salary unless they held office in the government, and Phineas had no money and no prospects of earning any. Nevertheless, he decided to take the risk. Through fortunate circumstances in Ireland, he had no difficulty in winning the seat, and in his middle twenties found himself the duly elected member for Loughshane, with his father's promise of an allowance of 250 pounds a year as long as the session lasted.

Apart from financial considerations, everything seemed in his favor. He was a tall and handsome man —honest and honorable, without a trace of either arrogance or conceit, and with a natural sweetness of manner which proved attractive to both men and women, and which made him a welcome guest in the houses of the great Whig aristocracy. Nevertheless, his very gifts provoked a certain amount of ill will. Mr. Rattler, the party whip, and especially Mr. Bonteen—a noisy gushing man, who was useful politically and who held office in the government as president of the Board of Trade—did not relish seeing Phineas make his easy way through doors that had been opened to them only as the tardy reward of laborious hack work. These men and others like them were not infrequently heard to say that they didn't think much of Mr. Phineas Finn.

The career of our hero during his first session in Parliament is recorded in *Phineas Finn* and I will not attempt to summarize the plot. Suffice it to say that after five years Phineas resigned his seat because he felt himself conscientiously unable to follow the party line in support of a particular piece of legislation. His friends were unanimous in thinking that his behavior was highly creditable to himself, but the Rattlers and Bonteens were confirmed in their belief that he was not a "safe" man politically. They regarded him, in short, as what we in the United States would call a mugwump. There have been times in my life when I too have been regarded as a mugwump. This is not the place to defend the attitude, or even to discuss it. I will say only this—there is no reward in life, however splendid, that will ever compensate you for a sense of the loss of your personal integrity.

The friends of Phineas were able to secure for him a small political office in Ireland, and he returned home and married his childhood sweetheart. Though he found his work dull and lacking in the glamour of service in Parliament, he did his best to conceal his feelings. During the course of the next two years his wife died in childbirth and his father also died, leaving him a small patrimony. Another general election was about to be held and Phineas decided that he would have one more fling at a political career for as long as his money lasted.

He won a seat in Parliament, this time for an English borough and after a spirited contest. His friends in London welcomed him with open arms, but it was soon apparent that the politicians were inclined to treat him with a certain coolness and distrust. More and more, he felt himself regarded as a political outsider, and more and more it seemed to him that Mr. Bonteen was the person chiefly responsible for this state of affairs. His pride would not let him utter any complaints, and his grievance grew the more because it had no outlet.

One evening Phineas went to his club, and arrived just in time to overhear Mr. Bonteen, who had obviously been drinking, say loudly: "Mr. Phineas Finn, or some such fellow as that, would be after her at once." Now the talk of London at the moment was the case of a certain Lady Eustace, a rich and pretty young woman who had married an unprincipled adventurer, a converted Bohemian Jew who passed under the name of the Rev. Joseph Emilius. She had soon left him and the couple were now engaged in two lawsuits—his to compel the return of his wife and to recover possession of her property, and hers to prove that at the time of the marriage Mr. Emilius already had a wife living in Prague and hence that the marriage was bigamous and void. Lady Eustace had taken refuge in the home of Mr. and Mrs. Bonteen, and Mr. Bonteen was in the act of attempting to secure proof of the alleged bigamy. Phineas guessed at once that Mr. Bonteen had been discussing the Eustace case, and that what he was saying was that if the bigamy were established some Phineas Finn would be after Lady Eustace for her money. He was very angry—not the less so because, while it was not in his character to offer marriage to a woman solely because she was rich, everybody knew that there could be no more fortunate destiny for him than to love and win a woman of wealth. He could not refrain from noticing Mr. Bonteen's remark. Words passed between them, rather insolent words on the part of Mr. Bonteen, but the entry of His Royal Highness, the Prince of Wales, put an inconclusive end to the quarrel. Later, when Phineas was leaving the club, he was followed by

Barrington Erle and another friend named Laurence Fitzgibbon. The three stopped at the door to talk over what had happened. Just then Mr. Bonteen came out alone. Phineas stepped back into the shadow, and Mr. Bonteen, after bidding the other two good night, went on to the eastward. With a laugh, Phineas took a life-preserver—that is, a club or bludgeon—out of the pocket of his overcoat, and made a gesture with it as though he were striking some enemy over the head. "By George," he said, "I do dislike that man." Let me pause here to give you my first piece of legal advice—never act and speak in that way, whether in jest or earnest. As soon as Phineas had spoken, he followed Mr. Bonteen down the street, at a distance of perhaps a couple of hundred yards.

On the next morning at seven o'clock, a superintendent of police called at the house of Mr. Gresham, the Prime Minister, and informed him that Mr. Bonteen, the president of the Board of Trade, had been murdered during the night. The body had been found not far from the club where the quarrel with Phineas had taken place, on the steps leading from the street to a dark passage running between the gardens of two great noblemen. The passage was almost as near a way as any from the club to Mr. Bonteen's house in St. James's Place; but the superintendent declared that gentlemen seldom used the passage after dark, and he was disposed to think that Mr. Bonteen must have been forced down the steps by the ruffian who had attacked him from the level above. The cause of death was three blows on the head by a blunt instrument. No weapon had been found.

It is one of the characteristics of Trollope's method

that he contrives to maintain interest without withholding the facts. "The reader need hardly be told," he remarks, "that, as regards this great offence, Phineas Finn was as white as snow. The maintenance of any doubt on that matter,—were it even desirable to maintain a doubt, —would be altogether beyond the power of the present writer. The reader has probably perceived from the first moment of the discovery of the body . . . that Mr. Bonteen had been killed by that ingenious gentleman, the Rev. Mr. Emilius, who found it to be worth his while to take the step with the view of suppressing his enemy's evidence as to his former marriage." So we know at once not only that Phineas was innocent but also who the guilty party was. The question remains what the police are going to think and what they are going to do.

As a matter of fact Mr. Emilius was their first suspect, because they knew about the enmity between him and Mr. Bonteen but knew nothing as yet about the quarrel between Mr. Bonteen and Phineas. Since his separation from Lady Eustace, Mr. Emilius had been in straitened circumstances and had moved to a shabby lodging house on Northumberland Street which was located close to the place where the murder was committed. The police took him into custody at once. He was found in bed in his lodgings between seven and eight o'clock in the morning, and while he seemed to be horror-struck when he heard of Mr. Bonteen's death, he openly expressed his joy. "He has endeavoured to ruin me, and has done me a world of harm. Why should I sorrow for him?" he said to the policeman, when rebuked for his inhumanity. Nevertheless, nothing was found to implicate him in the crime. The servant declared that he had gone to bed before eleven o'clock to her knowledge, and that he had not left the house afterwards. It appeared that he usually carried a latchkey, but that it was often borrowed from him by members of the family when it was known that he would not want it himself, —and that it had been so borrowed on this night. It was considered certain by those in the house that he had not gone out after he went to bed. Indeed, nobody had left the house after ten; but in accordance with his usual custom Mr. Emilius had sent down the key as soon as he had found that he would not want it, and it had been all night in the custody of the mistress of the establishment. His clothes were examined minutely for bloodstains, but without affording any evidence against him. No weapon was found in his possession. However, he remained in custody for the time being, though with no evidence against him except his acknowledged hostility to Mr. Bonteen.

At eleven o'clock in his private room at the Treasury Chambers, Mr. Gresham heard much more than the superintendent of police had been able to tell him in the first instance. At that time there were present with him two of his colleagues in the Cabinet, Lord Cantrip and the Duke of Omnium, three of his junior colleagues in the Government, Lord Fawn, Barrington Erle, and Laurence Fitzgibbon,—and Major Mackintosh, the chief of the London police. Major Mackintosh first reported on what steps had been taken in the case of Mr. Emilius. Both Erle and Fitzgibbon then described the quarrel at the club between Phineas and Mr. Bonteen, and described also the anger which Phineas had expressed against the wretched man as he stood talking at the club door. His gesture of vengeance was remembered and

repeated, though both of his friends expressed their
strongest conviction that the murder had not been
committed by him. But they told also of the life-
preserver which Phineas had shown them, as he took it
from the pocket of his outside coat. Then Lord Fawn
gave further evidence, which seemed to tell very hardly
upon Phineas. He also had been at the club, and had
left it just before Finn and the other two men had
clustered at the door. He had walked very slowly and
had seen nothing of Mr. Bonteen. However, as he was
in the act of crossing the street he was passed at a very
rapid pace by a man muffled in a topcoat, who made
his way straight toward the passage where Mr. Bonteen's
body was afterwards found. At the moment he had not
connected the person of the man who passed him with
any acquaintance of his own; but he now felt sure,
after what he had heard, that the man was Mr. Finn.
As he passed out of the club Finn was putting on his
overcoat, and Lord Fawn had observed the peculiarity
of the grey color. It was exactly a similar coat, only with
its collar raised, that had passed him in the street. The
man, too, was of Mr. Finn's height and build. He had
known Mr. Finn well, and the man stepped with Mr.
Finn's step. Major Mackintosh thought that Lord
Fawn's evidence was "very unfortunate as regarded Mr.
Finn."

"I'm damned if that idiot won't hang poor Phinny,"
said Fitzgibbon afterwards to Erle. "And yet I don't
believe a word of it."

"Fawn wouldn't lie for the sake of hanging Phineas
Finn," said Erle.

"No," answered Fitzgibbon, "I don't suppose he's
given to lying at all. He believes it all. But he's such a

muddle-headed fellow that he can get himself to believe anything. He's one of those men who always unconsciously exaggerate what they have to say for the sake of the importance it gives them."

Let me interject the remark that, as every trial lawyer knows, there are such witnesses. Whether Lord Fawn deserved what Fitzgibbon said about him will appear as the story proceeds.

On the basis of the evidence that I have just presented to you a superintendent of police accompanied by two constables called on Phineas at his lodgings and requested him to go with them to the police-office on Bow Street. The police took with them the life-preserver or bludgeon, the grey overcoat, and various other articles of wearing apparel. At the police-office Phineas, after repeated cautions, was permitted to tell his own story—which was to the effect that he had never overtaken Mr. Bonteen and had gone home to bed, taking the shortest way to his lodgings on Bruton Street. He had certainly been wearing the grey coat, but the collar of it had not been turned up. The coat was nearly new, and to the best of his knowledge the collar had never been turned up. He had carried the life-preserver for self-protection —partly because of an experience that he had once had on the London Streets and partly because of some recent commotion about attacks on pedestrians. He had purchased it about a month before, but even before its purchase he had been accustomed to carry some stick or bludgeon at night. It was true that words had passed between him and Mr. Bonteen at the club. It was also true that he had quarreled with Mr. Bonteen before this occasion and that he had bought the life-preserver since the commencement of the quarrel.

The statements made by Phineas were, of course, entirely voluntary and were made after the magistrate had heard the evidence produced by the police. This consisted of the testimony of five witnesses. Erle, Fitzgibbon, and Lord Fawn repeated the substance of the statements that they had made to the chief of police. A constable produced actual measurements and an estimate of times and speeds which demonstrated that the prisoner, after Erle and Fitzgibbon lost sight of him, would have had time to be in the place where Lord Fawn saw the man, supposing that Lord Fawn had walked at the rate of three miles an hour, and that Phineas had walked or run at twice that pace. Lord Fawn stated that he was walking very slowly—less, he thought, than three miles an hour, and that the man was hurrying very fast, not absolutely running, but going as he thought at quite double his own pace. Then two coats were shown to his lordship—the grey coat that Phineas had been wearing on the night of the murder, and a rough, thick, brown coat that the police had taken from the Rev. Mr. Emilius. Lord Fawn looked at the coats very attentively, and then said that the man he had seen had certainly not worn the brown coat. The night had been dark, but still he was sure that the coat had been grey. The collar had certainly been turned up. Finally, a tailor was produced who gave it as his opinion that Finn's coat had been lately worn with the collar raised. The magistrate, "with the profoundest regret," considered that the evidence was sufficient to require the temporary committal of Mr. Finn to Newgate. About a fortnight afterwards he was formally charged with the murder of Mr. Bonteen. In the meantime the police had released Mr. Emilius, though they continued to keep an eye on him.

It must be apparent to all of you by this time that our friend Phineas, innocent though we know him to have been, was in bad trouble and needed the services of a lawyer. On the advice of friends he consulted Mr. Wickerby, who was an active and experienced solicitor. I must interrupt my story for a moment to explain that in England the legal profession is divided into two parts —barristers and solicitors. A solicitor is a man of law, but not an advocate. A person who is about to be engaged in either civil or criminal litigation is required to go first to a solicitor, who guides his conduct by advice in the preliminary stages and then retains a barrister to try the case. The solicitor is permitted to sit with (or behind) the barrister in court but is not permitted to examine witnesses or to address the judge or jury. A barrister can never be retained by the litigants themselves. The only clients he can ever have are solicitors, whose clients, in turn, are the public. As a junior he may conduct a chamber practice consisting of giving opinions, drawing legal pleadings and the like. If, however, he "takes silk" and becomes a Queen's Counsel— King's Counsel, of course, if a King is on the throne— he wears a silk gown instead of a cotton one, but he must give up his chamber practice entirely and confine his activities to the art of advocacy. The times have been when a successful barrister in London made a lot of money. I have read recently that Charles Austin—who was a younger brother of John Austin, the political philosopher, and who practiced in the first part of the nineteenth century—earned 40,000 pounds a year when at the height of his reputation. At the old rate of exchange that would be not much less than $200,000.00, but allowing for the decrease in the purchasing power of the dollar it would amount to at least $1,000,000.00 today. I do not wish to discourage any of you who may be planning to make the law your career, but I must tell you plainly that none of you is ever going to make $1,000,000.00 a year—even before income tax and no matter where you may practice or how successful you may be. I could tell you why but the explanation would lead us too far afield.

The barrister retained by Mr. Wickerby was Mr. Chaffanbrass—"than whom," as Trollope assures us in not very flattering language, "no barrister living or dead ever rescued more culprits from the fangs of the law." In short, he was "an Old Bailey barrister"—that is, a barrister who specialized in the trial of criminal cases. He realized full well that in the opinion of some people the special branch of the profession into which he had chanced to fall was a very low one, and he was not sure whether, if the world were before him again, he would allow himself to drift into an exclusive practice in criminal courts. Nevertheless, as he confided to Mr. Wickerby, he often felt that his work touched the heart more nearly than did that of gentlemen who had to deal with matters of property and high social claims. There is much justification for this feeling. It so happens that I have never had a very extensive criminal practice—perhaps I never wanted it, though as to that I hardly know what the truth is—but I express the opinion that an honest criminal lawyer, and you may be sure that many of them exist, can and does play a great part in the administration of justice according to law.

Apart from his professional qualifications, Mr. Chaffanbrass was "an ugly, dirty old man." He proceeded with characteristic energy to prepare his client's defense.

I have said that Phineas had many loyal friends of both sexes. One of them was a rich and beautiful widow named Madame Marie Goesler. She was in her early thirties, had been born and reared on the continent of Europe, but had lived in England for many years and was received in the best English society.

It seemed to Madame Goesler that two important points ought to be investigated: (1) whether Mr. Emilius had procured a duplicate key by which he could have re-entered his lodgings on the night of the murder, assuming that he had left the house after having ostensibly gone to bed, and (2) whether there had been in the house a grey coat that he might have worn instead of the rough brown coat that the police had found. With these ideas in mind, she visited Mr. Emilius's landlady, Mrs. Meager, and dispensed sovereigns with a lavish hand. As to the key, she was able to learn nothing except that Mr. Emilius had made a journey to Prague not long before the murder had been committed and that during the period of his absence Mrs. Meager had been one key short. As to the coat, it appeared that Mr. Meager, the husband of the landlady, had been the owner of a grey coat which had been lying on the sofa on the night of the murder. He was a worthless scoundrel who was away from home a great part of the time. His custom was to buy a coat in November of each year and to pawn or sell it in the following April. Spring had come and the coat was no longer in his possession.

Madame Goesler presented the results of her investigation to Mr. Wickerby, the solicitor, but he was not impressed. "Next to an alibi that breaks down," he told her, "an unsuccessful attempt to affix the guilt on another party is the most fatal blow which a prisoner's counsel can inflict upon him." Generally speaking, I think this is a correct observation. Nevertheless, Mr. Wickerby undertook to try to locate the missing coat, and Madame Goesler started for Prague with a detective and an interpreter in search of evidence to show the making of a duplicate latchkey.

Madame Goesler had been a good deal discouraged in the course of her conversation with Mr. Wickerby. "Is there to be no defence, then?" she had asked, and Mr. Wickerby had assured her of the unprecedented number and eminence of the character witnesses who would be called to testify on the prisoner's behalf. I know what most of you are thinking—distinguished character witnesses may be all very well, but the real strength of the defense in this particular case lay in the candor and clarity of the testimony that Phineas would be able to give on his own behalf. You will be astonished, and I hope horrified, to learn that at the time Phineas was tried the law in both England and the United States was that a defendant in a criminal case was not permitted to testify. The rule was a monstrosity, and it cannot be successfully defended on any grounds. You will wish to know what arguments were ever advanced in the attempt to defend it. Well, it used to be said that if the defendant were guilty, he would be certain to perjure himself, and that the jury, knowing this, would not believe him even if he were innocent. I will not go to the trouble of demolishing these absurd arguments beyond pointing out that experience has demonstrated not only that lying is not as easy as Hamlet thought it was, but also that cross-examination, if conducted by a competent practitioner, is the best method ever devised for getting at the truth. It is a satisfaction to report that in Pennsylvania since 1887 and in England since 1898 the defendant has been fully competent to testify in all criminal cases. I wish I could add that the lawyers themselves were chiefly responsible for bringing about this reform. The contrary is the case. The person to whom most of the credit belongs is Jeremy Bentham, who was not a member of the legal profession. I do not agree with his philosophy of utilitarianism, but he deserves a statue in every courtroom in which the English language is spoken.

Two days before the trial began, a meeting was held in the private room of Mr. Wickerby. The persons present were Mr. Chaffanbrass, Mr. Wickerby himself, Mr. Wickerby's confidential clerk, Lord Fawn, Lord Fawn's solicitor, and a policeman. Mr. Wickerby had invited Lord Fawn to attend the meeting, with many protestations of regret as to the trouble thus imposed upon him, because the very important nature of the evidence to be given by him at the forthcoming trial seemed to render it expedient that some questions should be asked. At the trial, by the way, the attorney-general, Sir Gregory Grogram, who was leading the case for the prosecution, charged Mr. Chaffanbrass with having "tampered with" Lord Fawn as a witness. Mr. Chaffanbrass denied the charge with indignation, and Sir Gregory finally withdrew the objectionable word and substituted an assertion that Lord Fawn had been "indiscreetly questioned." Mr. Chaffanbrass denied this too, but the judge submitted to him that he *had* been indiscreet. I do not know what the law on this subject is in England, but in the United States the course fol-

lowed by Mr. Chaffanbrass would be regarded as correct
—even meticulously correct, since Lord Fawn's solicitor
was invited to attend the meeting, or at least permitted
to do so. The Canons of Professional Ethics of the
American Bar Association expressly provide that "a
lawyer may properly interview any witness or prospective witness for the opposing side in any civil or criminal
action without the consent of opposing counsel or
party." This seems to me to be a sound rule. After all,
the purpose of a trial at law is to find out the truth,
and I am unable to see any good reason why the service
of a subpoena on a prospective witness by one party
should render the witness immune from being questioned by representatives of the other party. Too often
what is known as legal ethics turns out, on proper
consideration, to be nothing but legal etiquette, without much logic to support it.

Mr. Wickerby had succeeded in locating the grey coat
which had formerly belonged to Mr. Meager, and he had
instructed Mr. Chaffanbrass that evidence would be
forthcoming, if needed, to prove that the coat was lying
on the night of the murder in a downstairs room in the
house in which Mr. Emilius was then lodging. Lord
Fawn was a dull, honest, conceited man, who was not
accustomed to having his statements called into question. "You see it is a grey coat," said Mr. Chaffanbrass,
not speaking at all in the tone which Mr. Wickerby's
note had induced Lord Fawn to expect.

"It is grey," said Lord Fawn.

Mr. Chaffanbrass went on.

"You don't think the coat the man wore when you
saw him was a big coat like that? You think he wore a
little coat?"

"He wore a grey coat," said Lord Fawn.

"I don't think Lord Fawn should be asked any more questions on the matter till he gives his evidence in court," said his lordship's solicitor.

"A man's life depends on it," said Mr. Chaffanbrass. "Lord Fawn doesn't want to hang Mr. Finn, if Mr. Finn be not guilty."

"God forbid!" said his lordship.

Then Mr. Scruby, Mr. Wickerby's clerk, put on the coat and walked quickly about the room in it. He was a stout, thick-set little man, nearly half a foot shorter than Phineas Finn. "Is that at all like the figure?" asked Mr. Chaffanbrass.

"I think it is like the figure," said Lord Fawn. When pressed about the likeness, he explained:

"When Mr. Scruby hurries down the room in that way he looks as the man looked when he was hurrying under the lamp-post."

Lord Fawn's solicitor interrupted again, but Mr. Chaffanbrass had no more questions to ask. He told Mr. Scruby to take off the coat and give it to the policeman for safekeeping. "I understand Lord Fawn to say that the man's figure was about the same as yours," he remarked. "My client, I believe, stands about twelve inches taller. Thank you, my lord;—we shall get the truth at last, I don't doubt."

Lord Fawn went home very much afraid of Mr. Chaffanbrass.

In spite of the encouraging nature of the interview with Lord Fawn, Mr. Wickerby and Mr. Chaffanbrass were separately of the opinion that Phineas was guilty. They never discussed this question. Naturally enough, Phineas, though incompetent to testify, wanted to have an interview with Mr. Chaffanbrass before the trial began; and Mr. Chaffanbrass reluctantly granted his request.

"Of course he wants to tell his own story," said Mr. Wickerby.

Mr. Chaffanbrass protested.

"But I don't want to hear his own story. What good will his own story do me? He'll tell me either one of two things. He'll swear he didn't murder the man . . . which can have no effect upon me one way or the other; or else he'll say that he did,—which would cripple me altogether. . . . In nineteen cases out of twenty a man tried for murder in this country committed the murder for which he is tried."

Mr. Wickerby pointed out that there really seemed to be a doubt in the present case.

"I dare say," said Mr. Chaffanbrass. "If there be only nineteen guilty out of twenty, there must be one innocent; and why not Mr. Phineas Finn?"

The interview between attorney and client took place, and Mr. Chaffanbrass was impressed in spite of himself. After he and Mr. Wickerby had left the prison, he said: "I never did,—and I never will,—express an opinion of my own as to the guilt or innocence of a client till after the trial is over. But I have sometimes felt as if I would give the blood out of my veins to save a man. I never felt in that way more strongly than I do now."

Every lawyer worth his salt has felt in that way at some time during the course of his professional career.

The behavior and remarks of Mr. Chaffanbrass raise, of course, the perennial question of whether a lawyer is ethically justified in defending a man whom he believes to be guilty. Here again I can quote the Canons of

Professional Ethics in defense of Mr. Chaffanbrass: "It is the right of a lawyer to undertake the defense of a person accused of crime, regardless of his personal opinion as to the guilt of the accused; otherwise innocent persons, victims only of suspicious circumstances, might be denied proper defense. Having undertaken such defense, the lawyer is bound, by all fair and honorable means, to present every defense that the law of the land permits, to the end that no person may be deprived of life or liberty, but by due process of law."

In my opinion the canon is correct, but in order to avoid any misunderstanding I must call your attention to two other principles of professional ethics. The first is that no matter what the actual state of mind of a lawyer may be, he should *never* assert in argument his personal belief in his client's innocence or in the justice of his cause.

The second principle must be considered only in the rare case where an accused person has made a private confession of guilt to his lawyer. There is authority for the statement that under these circumstances the lawyer, unless he suspects mental derangement or some other unusual condition, should advise his client to plead guilty and should withdraw from the case unless the client follows his advice. It so happens that this represents my own view. However, there is likewise authority for the statement that in the case supposed the lawyer may properly represent the accused, provided he limits his activities to seeing to it that the defendant is accorded all his legal and constitutional rights. If a lawyer accepts employment under these conditions, he may not call his client to testify to a story that he knows to be untrue, he may not present an alibi that he knows to be untrue, and he may not make any argument that might suggest the guilt of an innocent person. In a word, he is "crippled," as Mr. Chaffanbrass expressed it. The Earl of Birkenhead presented still another solution in addressing the American Bar Association in the year 1923. "If," he said, "you take the extremest case of all, the case where it has been put at its strongest against the ethical situation of our profession, the case where a confession has been made by a prisoner to an advocate—I would meet that case without hesitation. . . . I would meet that by saying, 'You are not to be the judge of whether that confession is made under an aberration, under a delusion, in hysteria; you are to put the whole facts of that case as those facts are known to you before the jury and before the judge, and they and not you are to decide as to the facts that have been proved, and as to the reliability of that which has been admitted.' " The problem is perhaps complicated by the fact that in England a barrister is ordinarily required to accept every case that is offered to him. He is "a cabman on the Rank bound to answer the first hail." The law is otherwise in the United States.

The trial of Phineas Finn was followed with the closest attention by his friends and also by the public generally. You are already familiar with the evidence that the attorney-general produced. Mr. Chaffanbrass gave Lord Fawn a very bad half hour on cross-examination. His lordship had evidently made up his mind to express as few opinions as possible. On direct-examination he had stated that he could not identify Phineas as the man he had seen on the street, but that he thought, so far as he could judge, there was not much difference in the height of the two men. On cross-examination Mr. Chaffanbrass asked him almost at once whether Phineas was not a very tall man. Very foolishly Lord Fawn declined to give an opinion. He had known Phineas well, though not intimately, and the prisoner was then standing before him in the dock. When Mr. Chaffanbrass offered to have Phineas stand down so that Lord Fawn could examine him, his lordship finally admitted that he was a very tall man. "Now we shall get on like a house on fire," said Mr. Chaffanbrass. However, as Trollope tells us, the house did not burn very quickly. Lord Fawn could not remember what words he had used in testifying before the magistrate, and refused to refresh his recollection by reading a report of his testimony that had appeared in the *Times*. That testimony, he said, had been based chiefly on the color of the coat worn by the man who had passed him on the street, and on the fact that there had been a quarrel between Phineas and Mr. Bonteen. Thereupon Mr. Chaffanbrass asked Mr. Scruby to put on the coat that had formerly belonged to Mr. Meager. The cross-examination of Lord Fawn was interrupted for a moment, and it was shown that Mr. Scruby had been accurately measured on the previous day and that he was five feet eight inches tall. The coat seemed to fit him well. When cross-examination was resumed, Lord Fawn was at last driven to admit that at the meeting in Mr. Wickerby's chambers he had acknowledged a certain resemblance between Mr. Scruby and the mysterious stranger and that, in some faint ambiguous fashion, he acknowledged it in his present evidence.

This is as good a place as any to tell you that the case against Phineas seems to me to have been at all times a very weak one—so weak, indeed, that even if Lord

Fawn had not been shaken on cross-examination the judge would perhaps have thought it his duty to direct the jury to acquit the defendant. But Lord Fawn had been severely shaken, and my guess is that when he stepped down from the witness box Phineas was out of danger. He did not know it, and I doubt whether he ever fully realized the debt of gratitude that he owed to Mr. Chaffanbrass.

Mr. Chaffanbrass and Phineas now became the beneficiaries of two pieces of luck. The investigation of Madame Goesler had proved to be a brilliant success, and after Mr. Chaffanbrass had put in his character evidence he was able to call a Bohemian blacksmith who testified through an interpreter that he had made a pass-key from a mold supplied by Mr. Emilius. It was also shown that the key was one that would open Mr. Meager's door in Northumberland Street. I question whether this evidence was legally admissible. After all, the possession of a duplicate key by Mr. Emilius was a matter entirely collateral to the guilt of Phineas Finn. If Mr. Emilius had such a key on the night of the murder, he *might* have left his lodgings and returned to them unobserved, but there was no evidence that he *had* left them.

The second piece of luck occurred when a small boy, playing in one of the gardens abutting on the passage at the entrance of which Mr. Bonteen's body had been discovered, found a loaded bludgeon encased in leather, which experts declared was not of English manufacture. I think this *was* admissible evidence, as tending to raise a reasonable doubt of the defendant's guilt, and I think further that the police were remiss in not having found the bludgeon in the first place.

After the evidence had been completed, the judge charged the jury that while he thought the trial had been fully justified in the first instance, nevertheless, even if nothing had arisen to point to the possibility of guilt in another man, he would have found himself bound in duty to explain to them that the thread of the evidence against Mr. Finn had been incomplete—or, he would rather say, that the weight of it had been, to his judgment, insufficient. "Gentlemen," he concluded, "I think you will find no difficulty in acquitting the prisoner of the murder laid to his charge." Thereupon the jurymen put their heads together and the foreman, without half a minute's delay, declared that they were unanimous and that they found the prisoner not guilty. "And we are of opinion," said the foreman, "that Mr. Finn should not have been put upon his trial on such evidence as has been brought before us."

So Phineas was triumphantly acquitted. I hope you have been enough interested to want information on one or two points. What happened to Mr. Emilius? He was never prosecuted. Lord Fawn had been so much humiliated and discredited by his experience in court that he was no longer willing to identify anybody—he would have refused to identify his mother's butler if he had met the man on the street in broad daylight. What happened to Phineas Finn? He married Madame Goesler, of course. She had plenty of money, and on that account he was able to remain in Parliament without holding office. I have never been able to learn whether they had any children.

Shakespeare and the Law

LET me begin by telling you that on the subject of Shakespeare I am completely orthodox. I am persuaded that the author of the plays, the poems, and the sonnets was the first son and third child of John Shakespeare and Mary (Arden) Shakespeare, his wife, who were residents of the town of Stratford, in England, during the latter half of the sixteenth century. At that time there were many towns in England called Stratford. As all of you know, the Stratford in which John and Mary Shakespeare lived was the one in Warwickshire on the banks of the river Avon.

It has frequently been said that we have very little information about Shakespeare's life. There is a sense in which this statement is correct, and another sense in which it is incorrect. Of course we know less about Shakespeare than about a Victorian poet like Browning, but we know more about him than about any Elizabethan poet or playwright, with the possible exception of Ben Jonson.

We know the place of his birth but not the exact date of it. The parish register records the fact that he was baptized on April 26, 1564. He died at Stratford fifty-two years later, on the 23rd of April, and there is a tradition that he died on his birthday. It will appear as this lecture proceeds that I am skeptical about most of the traditions concerning him, but I am inclined to view this one with benevolence. The 23rd of April is St. George's Day, and St. George is the patron saint of England. It is pleasant to think that England's greatest poet and one of the most patriotic Englishmen who ever lived was born and died on the day set apart to do honor to his country's patron saint.

The first solidly established fact that we have about Shakespeare after his baptism is that when he was eighteen years of age he married a woman named Anne Hathaway. She had been brought up in the neighborhood of Stratford and was his senior by eight years. Their first child, a daughter who was named Susanna, was born about six months after the marriage took place. Some people think that William seduced Anne; others that Anne seduced William; while still others, most of whom belong to the group sometimes called "Shakespearean idolaters," believe that the parties had entered into what was known as a pre-contract and hence that no misbehavior took place. Nobody knows what the turth is, but I cannot help remarking that the last conjecture seems to me the least probable of the three.

The idolaters believe, though I am afraid they would not admit it, that Shakespeare was never guilty of any misbehavior, and never made any mistakes, either metrical or factual; that in the plays that are wholly his all the bad lines are the results of faulty manuscripts or poor proofreading; that in the plays in which he had a collaborator he wrote all the good lines and the other man all the bad ones; and that the bawdy in the plays comes from the ad-libbing of foul-mouthed actors. Dr. Furness, the editor of the *Variorum Shakespeare* and an idolater if ever there was one, was delighted in his edition of *The Winter's Tale* to demonstrate, at least to his own satisfaction, that Bohemia once had a sea-coast, so that the landfall which enters into the plot of that play might actually have occurred. This throws no light, however, on the striking clock in *Julius Caesar*, Hector quoting Aristotle in *Troilus and Cressida*, Hamlet studying at a university that was not founded until five hundred years after his time, pistols in the age of Henry IV, and cannon in the age of King John. Ben Jonson said that he honored Shakespeare's memory "on this side idolatry as much as any." So do I, but, like Jonson, I try to stay on this side.

As Dr. Gogarty has written: "There's no good love without good luck." All the evidence seems to show that Shakespeare's marriage was not a lucky one. During more than half of the period of about thirty-four years between the celebration of the marriage and the date of Shakespeare's death he and Anne did not live together, or at least did not live together regularly. I cannot tell you how deep their estrangement was. A recent critic has suggested that Anne, who had been brought up in a Puritan family, was perhaps prejudiced against the acting profession. She certainly was if she followed the Puritan line, which denounced actors as apes, hell-hounds, vipers, minotaurs, painted sepulchres, dogs and caterpillars.

When Shakespeare came to make his will he did not mention Anne by name, but by an interlineation in the final draft he left her his "second best bed with the furniture." Some people find in this bequest a sign of settled ill will on his part. Other people think that Anne was sentimental about the bed and asked to have it. Here again, nobody knows what the truth is.

After Shakespeare's marriage the next solidly established fact about him is that in 1592 he was an actor in London and a playwright of sufficient prominence to arouse the enmity of the dying Greene, who called him an "upstart crow." So far as I know, these are the only hard words about Shakespeare that have come down to us from his contemporaries. Henry Chettle, the printer who edited Greene's manuscript, afterwards expressed regret that he had not used his own discretion and moderated the language of the passage about the upstart crow. He was as sorry he had not done so, he wrote, as if the original fault had been his.

When Shakespeare left Stratford and why he left are matters of conjecture. Anne had borne him twins in 1585. There were no other children, and it is generally supposed that he took up his residence in London not long after the birth of the twins. As to his reasons for leaving Stratford, the most popular explanation is to be found in the deer-stealing story, which was first written down by the Rev. Richard Davies late in the seventeenth century, and was repeated and embellished by Rowe. According to this story, Shakespeare stole deer from "a park that belonged to Sir Thomas Lucy, of Charlecote, near Stratford," and "was prosecuted by that gentleman . . . to that degree that he was obliged to leave his business and family in Warwickshire for some time and shelter himself in London." A serious objection to this legend is that the Lucy family did not keep a deer park in the sixteenth century. Edmund

Malone, who has been justly called "the first and one of the greatest of the real Shakespearean scholars," remarked bitterly that Rowe had made eleven statements about Shakespeare's life and that eight of them were demonstrably false.

The period of six or seven years between Shakespeare's departure from Stratford and the upstart crow reference in 1592 is the most controversial one in the poet's life. We are without any actual information, and the wildest guesses have been resorted to. Aubrey reported that "he had been in his younger years a schoolmaster in the country." There is a story that he found employment in a printing office, and another that he served as a lawyer's clerk. Dr. Furness quotes an authority in order to show that his knowledge of seamanship as disclosed in the first scene of *The Tempest* was so accurate that, in the absence of experience, he "must have acquired it by conversation with some of the most skillful seamen of that time." Some critics have supposed that he visited the continent of Europe. I feel sure that I could extend the list of conjectures, but I will end with the legend that he was employed for a time to hold the horses of people of fashion who came to the theater on horseback, and that he performed this task with so much dexterity that he was obliged, before being promoted to a higher employment within doors, to train up boys to assist him. A modern scholar has summed up the evidence in support of this story by saying that "it was recounted by 'a gentleman, who heard it' from 'Dr. Newton, the late editor of Milton,' who was 'told it' by Pope, who had it from Rowe, who had it from Betterton, who had it from D'Avenant"; and that Dr. Johnson added "the very words the horseholders used: 'I am Shakespeare's boy, Sir.' " You may believe any of these stories that you happen to like, but you can hardly believe all of them because there is not enough time at our disposal.

D'Avenant, by the way, who was only ten years old when Shakespeare died, lived to become poet laureate of England. His mother was the wife of a man who had kept a tavern on High Street in Oxford, where it is said that Shakespeare was accustomed to break his journey between Stratford and London. She was "a very beautiful woman of good wit and conversation," and when the poet laureate was in his cups he used to drop hints that he was Shakespeare's bastard son. You may believe this one too if you are so minded.

Beginning with 1592 we have comparatively plain sailing. For almost twenty years Shakespeare was a resident of London. He paid regular city taxes and we know some of the places where he lodged. Early in his career he published two poems, not very good poems by the way: *Venus and Adonis* and *The Rape of Lucrece*. They were favorably received but he never published anything else. He belonged to a company of actors successively known as "the Lord Chamberlain's men," "Lord Hunsdon's men," and, in the reign of James, "the King's men." He was still acting as late as 1608. In addition, he wrote plays for his company at the average rate of almost two a year. As early as 1597 he had accumulated enough money to purchase "New Place," the second largest house in Stratford. In 1610, being then forty-six years of age, he retired to Stratford where he died six years afterwards. There is a legend that he, Drayton and Ben Jonson "had a merry meeting, and it seems drank too hard, for Shakespeare died of a fever there contracted." A physician has expressed the opinion that if the merry meeting took place angina pectoris would be a more likely result than a fever.

I have told you in summary form all there is to know about Shakespeare's life, but it is obvious that I have not told you all there is to know about Shakespeare. There remain the poems, the sonnets, and the thirty-seven plays comprising what is known as the Shakespearean canon. It is a fascinating adventure to attempt to determine from these writings what manner of man their author was. A distinguished critic has cautioned us that Shakespeare "is not to be found in the plays themselves." This seems to me little better than nonsense. In drawing conclusions about Shakespeare from the plays we must be wary, of course, but I take it to be certain that every creator (even the greatest creator of all) leaves something of himself in whatever he creates.

With these considerations in mind, I propose to set down some of the characteristics of the figure that seems to me to emerge from an evaluation of all the evidence at our disposal.

We are confronted, I think, with a modest and companionable man who cared nothing whatever about posthumous fame; a philosophic skeptic, though more sympathetic toward Catholicism than toward Protestantism; a lover of country life and especially of flowers; more moved by music than by either painting or sculpture; a drinker but not a smoker; conspicuously weak in mathematics; fond of horses and tolerant toward cats but disliking and distrusting dogs; interested throughout his whole life in Roman history and particularly in the career of Julius Caesar; a passionate nationalist and patriot, though strangely indifferent to the long struggle of the English people to achieve civil liberty. I have reserved for the last the only one of my conclusions that is directly related to the subject of this evening's lecture —I think Shakespeare was generally contemptuous of the law, lawyers, and legal procedure.

In recounting some of the legends concerned with Shakespeare's youth I included a conjecture that he had once served as a lawyer's clerk. The only piece of external evidence ever offered in support of this conjecture is an allusion by Thomas Nashe to an "English Seneca" who had left "the trade of Noverint" (i.e., law-scrivener) "and was capable of writing whole Hamlets." Nearly all scholars now agree that this allusion was not to Shakespeare but to Thomas Kyd, the son and assistant of a law-scrivener and the author of an early *Hamlet* which was one of the sources of Shakespeare's play. With this supposed piece of evidence out of the way, nothing is left except whatever internal evidence may be found in the plays themselves.

The authority most frequently quoted in support of the claim that Shakespeare possessed extensive legal knowledge is Lord Campbell, an English judge of the nineteenth century who served as Chief Justice of the Queen's Bench and afterwards as Lord Chancellor. As the Encyclopedia Britannica puts it with uncharacteristic acidity, "the unlucky dream of literary fame troubled Lord Campbell's leisure." In 1849 he produced a set of books called *The Lives of the Lord Chancellors* which is supposed to be found on the shelves of every lawyer. The books are not only dull but also so grossly prejudiced that Sir Charles Wetherell was moved to refer to their author as "my noble and biographical friend who has added a new terror to death."

Two years before his own death, which occurred in 1861, Lord Campbell published a book called *Shakespeare's Legal Requirements*. His conclusion was that "to Shakespeare's law, lavishly as he propounds it, there can neither be demurrer nor bill of exceptions, nor writ of error." The lawyers in the audience will know what this means, and to the laymen I will say only that when you are dealing with law like that you are dealing with law of the sort that the Supreme Court of the United States is presumed to lay down.

Now when a lawyer is about to express disagreement with a judge he always begins by saying: "With the greatest respect"—a form of words which is, I suppose, intended to avoid irritating the judge beyond the inescapable minimum. In the case of a judge who has been in his grave for almost a hundred years the precaution seems unnecessary, but the habit is too deeply ingrained for me to abandon it. With the greatest respect, then, I differ with Lord Campbell. I think he overestimated Shakespeare's real legal knowledge, and at the same time greatly underestimated his enormous acquisitive powers. Lord Campbell's industry discovered less than a hundred legal allusions in the plays. The correct number is about three hundred, but the great weight of critical opinion, both lay and professional, supports the statement of Sir Sidney Lee that the law thus presented is "a mingled skein of accuracy and inaccuracy," and that "the errors are far too numerous and important to justify on sober inquiry the plea of technical experience." My own view of the matter is that Shakespeare simply kept his ears open, as his custom was. No better ears for picking up information ever existed. When the lawyers talked nonsense he was quick to notice and deride, but when they talked sense he paid no attention whatever.

Let me illustrate by referring to two of the most famous scenes in Shakespeare's plays—the graveyard scene in *Hamlet* and the trial scene in *The Merchant of Venice*. I must approach the graveyard by way of an actual piece of litigation.

One of the notable lawsuits of the Elizabethan era was the case of *Hales v. Petit*. Sir James Hales was one of the judges who condemned the unfortunate Lady Jane Grey. Whether because of remorse, as some people supposed, or for some other reason, he lost his reason and came to his death by walking into a river near his home at Canterbury. A coroner's jury having returned a verdict of suicide, the estates of Sir James were forfeited to the Crown. His widow brought an action with the object of saving from the forfeiture a lease which she and her husband had held as joint tenants. She claimed that the lease had vested in her as a joint tenant in her husband's lifetime, and that her right of survivorship sprang up immediately after her husband's death, and took priority over the forfeiture.

According to Plowden's report of the case, Sergeant Walshe, representing the defendant, argued that "the act of self-destruction consists of three parts. The first is the imagination, which is a reflexion or meditation of the man's mind whether or not it be convenient to destroy himself and in what way it may be done; the second is the resolution, which is the determination of the mind to destroy himself and to do it in this or that particular way; the third is the perfection, which is the execution of what the mind has resolved to do. And this perfection consists of two parts, viz. the beginning and the end. The beginning is the doing of that act which causes the death, and the end is the death, which is only a sequel of the act. Then, here the act of Sir James Hales, which is evil and the cause of his death is the throwing of himself in the water, and the death is but the sequel thereof."

Throughout the argument there was much discussion as to whether Sir James was the "agent" or the "patient" —that is, whether he went to the water or the water came to him. Judge Browne delivered judgment from the bench as follows: "Sir James Hales was dead. And how came he by his death? It may be answered, by drowning. And who drowned him? Sir James Hales. And when did he drown him? In his lifetime. So that Sir James Hales being alive caused Sir James Hales to die, and the act of the living was the death of the dead man. And for this offence it is reasonable to punish the living man, who committed the offence, and not the dead man."

I have difficulty in understanding from this language what the decision of the court was. According to Blackstone the widow lost her case, but Professor Wilson in his edition of *Hamlet* seems to think that she won it.[1]

Let us turn now to the case of Ophelia who, like Sir James Hales, lost her reason and committed suicide by drowning. Over her grave the first gravedigger propounds to his colleague the question of whether she

---

[1] I have examined the report and my conclusion is that Blackstone was right.

ought to have a Christian burial. His comrade says yes, because the coroner had sat on her and had found it so. But the first gravedigger is not satisfied with this answer. He develops the subject along the very lines of Sergeant Walshe's argument: "For here lies the point: If I drown myself wittingly it argues an act: and an act hath three branches; it is to act, to do, to perform; argal, she drowned herself wittingly." He then proceeds in the manner of Judge Browne: "Here lies the water: good; and here stands the man: good. If the man goes to the water and drowns himself, it is will he, nill he, he goes— mark you that; but if the water come to him and drown him, he drowns not himself; argal, he that is not guilty of his own death shortens not his own life." I think no reasonable person can doubt that these are parodies of the pretentious nonsense talked in *Hales v. Petit,* and that Shakespeare was amusing himself at the expense of what he called "old father antic the law." [2]

So much for the lawyers talking nonsense.

The Merchant of Venice is one of Shakespeare's most charming comedies—so charming, indeed, that we are inclined to forget that it is altogether without morals. In spite of some modern attempts at a contrary interpretation, which I sympathize with but cannot accept, Shylock remains the villain of the piece. He was a wicked and revengeful man, who sought by indirection to bring about the death of his enemy Antonio. Nevertheless, he had very good grounds for hating Antonio. He puts his case almost as briefly as I could do it and much more eloquently:

[2] Sir John Hawkins, the friend of Dr. Johnson, was the first person to call attention to the parallels between the cases of Sir James Hales and Ophelia.

"Signior Antonio, many a time and oft
In the Rialto you have rated me
About my moneys and my usances:
Still have I borne it with a patient shrug;
For sufferance is the badge of all our tribe.
You call me misbeliever, cut-throat dog,
And spit upon my Jewish gaberdine,
And all for use of that which is mine own.
Well then, it now appears you need my help:
Go to, then; you come to me, and you say
'Shylock, we would have moneys:' you say so;
You, that did void your rheum upon my beard,
And foot me as you spurn a stranger cur
Over your threshold; moneys is your suit.
What should I say to you? Should I not say
'Hath a dog money? is it possible
A cur can lend three thousand ducats?' or
Shall I bend low and in a bondman's key,
With bated breath and whispering humbleness
Say this,—
'Fair sir, you spit on me on Wednesday last;
You spurn'd me such a day; another time
You call'd me dog; and for these courtesies
I'll lend you thus much moneys'?"

Now what does Antonio say in answer to these
charges? He says they are all true and that he has no
regrets—he is likely to call Shylock a dog in the future
if he happens to be in the mood, to spit on him again,
and to spurn him too. If this is a picture of a Christian
gentleman, I can only say that I would not wish to
include him in the number of my friends.

Shylock had a beautiful young daughter named

Jessica. Although she could talk poetry like an angel when the occasion required, her real character was far from angelic. She was unhappy at home and decided to run away with Bassanio's friend Lorenzo, who boasted of his conquest in a not very mannerly way. When she eloped she stole from her father all the cash she could get her hands on, and also jewelry including a turquoise ring that her deceased mother, Leah, had given to her father before they were married. If we are to believe Tubal, this heartless juvenile delinquent exchanged the ring for a monkey while she was on her wedding trip.

Bassanio was a prodigal young man, who had wasted his substance in riotous living. His chief care, as he explained to Antonio, was to come fairly off from his great debts, and he concluded that the only way in which he could do it was to marry a rich wife. Therefore, he made up his mind to pay court to Portia, who, as he was also careful to explain, was "richly left," "fair," and "of wondrous virtues." You will notice the order in which he enumerated her excellencies. Her beauty no doubt added to the zest of the adventure, but I feel sure that Bassanio would have married her if she had been as ugly as the witches in *Macbeth*.

I have left Portia to the last, because she has come to be regarded, almost by acclamation, as one of the most delightful of Shakespeare's heroines. I do not altogether share this sense of admiration. In my opinion the quality-of-mercy speech scarcely deserves the praise that has been lavished upon it. If we are to continue to require school children to memorize passages from Shakespeare, I can think of twenty speeches containing better poetry. At all events Portia did not take her own advice to heart. She delivered a homily to Shylock on the subject of mercy, but showed no mercy to him when the tables were turned. Moreover, she had at times an unctuous manner of speaking that I find rather disagreeable. Not long after welcoming Lorenzo and Jessica to her house she remarked smugly:

> "I never did repent for doing good,
>   Nor shall not now,"

and added:

> "This comes too near the praising of myself."

I think it did come too near. Even in the eloquent speech beginning "You see me, Lord Bassanio, where I stand," she described herself in glowing terms as one not so old but she might learn, not so dull but she could learn, and having a "gentle spirit." I suggest that it would have been better to let Bassanio discover these good qualities for himself. A friend of mine, a woman, was once asked at a dinner party what character in fiction she would choose to marry if the choice were open to her. She answered that she could not decide between Mr. Rochester and Bagheera the panther. If a like question were propounded to me, Rosalind would be at the top of the list or close to it, but Portia would be quite far down.

In putting together *The Merchant of Venice* Shakespeare skillfully blended three plots—the casket plot, the ring plot, and the pound of flesh plot. This evening we are concerned only with the pound of flesh.

Antonio, being in need of money to finance Bassanio's courtship of Portia, borrowed three thousand ducats from Shylock on the security of his "single bond"—

which means, I take it, a bond without sureties. The penalty of the bond was that if it was not paid at maturity, Shylock could claim "a pound of flesh, to be by him cut off nearest the merchant's heart." When the form of this extraordinary instrument was proposed by Shylock, he assured Antonio that the whole thing was done "in a merry sport" and asked with apparent candor what he would gain by the exaction of the forfeiture. Bassanio protested faintly, but Antonio felt sure that his argosies would return in time and signed on the dotted line. When the bond fell due he could not pay it and Shylock went into court in order to collect his pound of flesh.

Lord Campbell gave it as his opinion that the trial was "duly conducted according to the strict rules of legal procedure." It is hard to say what he meant by this statement. Shylock was rich, and Bassanio, who had succeeded in marrying Portia by this time, had all her fortune behind him. Nevertheless, it never occurred to either of them to get a lawyer. The Duke was the judge, but he was a judge not learned in the law. He remitted the case to a juris-consult of Padua, who sent Portia as his deputy disguised as a young doctor of Rome. This way of trying a case by referring it to a doctor of laws came from Shakespeare's Italian original. Some such procedure was prevalent in the Middle Ages in Spain and Italy, and a modern traveler has reported the existence of a similar procedure in Nicaragua.

Portia, who came into court fully prepared to defeat and humiliate Shylock and who was apparently indifferent to the feelings of Antonio, began by ruling that the bond was lawful and that Shylock could enforce the forfeiture. However, when he was about to put his knife to its intended use she stopped him with an outrageous quibble. The bond, she said, was silent about blood, and if in the course of cutting he shed as much as one drop of Antonio's blood his lands and goods would be confiscated to the state of Venice. Shylock was understandingly horrified. "Is *that* the law?" he exclaimed. Portia assured him that it was and that he himself should see the "act." She did not show it to him, however, and I don't believe there was any such act.

But Portia had not finished her sport with Shylock. She then went on to explain that he had violated another law, which provided that if an alien directly or indirectly sought the life of any citizen the injured party could seize half of his goods; that the other half went to "the privy coffer of the state"; and that the offender's life lay at the mercy of the Duke. Here Shakespeare got mixed up about the two halves of Shylock's goods, as he nearly always got mixed up when he had to deal with figures.[3] As a result it is impossible to tell exactly what Shylock had left after Antonio and the Duke had finished making magnanimous speeches. Only three points are clear: (1) Shylock had to become a Christian, (2) he had to execute a "deed of gift" whereby Lorenzo and Jessica would receive his entire estate at his death, and (3) Antonio or Bassanio, depending on how they settled their accounts between them, got three thousand ducats of Shylock's money gratis.

The trial scene presents two legal questions—a big

[3] Another example is to be found in the terms of the wager made by the King on the outcome of the fencing match between Hamlet and Laertes. Dr. Johnson, one of the most candid of critics, remarked simply: "This wager I do not understand."

question and a little one. I will deal with the little question first. Was there any merit in Portia's ruling about the shedding of blood? According to the construction that she adopted, if a man contracts for leave to cut a slice of melon, he will be deprived of the benefit of his contract unless he has stipulated, in so many words, for the incidental spilling of the juice.[4] It is true that in the law of real life judges have sometimes resorted to quibbles in an attempt, either conscious or unconscious, to escape from the consequences of a bad law. Nevertheless, I must give it as my opinion that if Shylock was entitled to his pound of flesh, he was entitled to shed as much blood as became necessary to enforce the forfeiture. But was Shylock entitled to his pound of flesh? This, of course, is the big question.

Now it so happens that one of the burning legal issues in the England in which Shakespeare lived was what ought to be done in cases involving penalties in bonds. The controversy arose between the courts of common law and the courts of equity, and was concerned with penalties not payable in pounds of flesh but in those other and more familiar pounds consisting of twenty shillings. In order to make the issue clear I must tell you something about the role played by the courts of equity in English jurisprudence, and about the early English law on the subject of usury.

The office of chancellor goes back at least to the reign of Edward the Confessor. In early days the chancellor was always an ecclesiastic, and this practice continued, with only rare exceptions, up until Shakespeare's time.

---

[4] The illustration of the melon comes from Haynes, *Outlines of Equity*.

Sir Thomas More—perhaps I should say Saint Thomas More, for he has recently been canonized—who served as chancellor under Henry VIII was the first lawyer to hold the office in more than a hundred years. Originally, the chancellor was, I suppose, little more than royal chaplain or confessor to the king. Anyway, it was said that he was the keeper of the king's conscience. According to English theory the king is the fountainhead of justice, and when appeals were made to him to mitigate the rigor of the law in particular cases, the chancellor told him what he ought to do. "This is he," wrote John of Salisbury who died in 1180, "who cancels the evil laws of the realm, and makes equitable the commands of a pious prince."

John of Salisbury really anticipated the jurisdiction afterwards asserted by the courts of equity. As time went on the power and dignity of the chancellor became greatly increased. He set up courts in which he heard and decided cases of particular types. In doing so he claimed to administer not the law of the land, but something better—the natural law written by God on the hearts and consciences of men. I hope to have something more to say about natural law tomorrow evening. The culmination of the chancellor's claims came when he began issuing injunctions in certain cases to restrain the execution of judgments by the courts of common law that he regarded as morally wrong. As might be expected, these injunctions set off a bitter controversy between the law courts and the equity courts. The struggle began before Shakespeare's birth, continued during his lifetime, and did not end until after his death. In the end the chancellor prevailed in certain fields of the law and was defeated in others. For present purposes we are concerned only with the issue between the parties so far as it related to the subject of usury.

As I am sure most of you know, in the Middle Ages the word usury meant interest of any kind and not, as at present, exorbitant interest. Both in England, and almost universally on the continent of Europe as well, the laws prohibited usury—chiefly on the authority of the Old Testament and a foolish saying of the usually wise Aristotle that money is a barren thing which does not breed. So is a house a barren thing, but so far as I know nobody has ever seen any objection to the collection of rent. As is the case with most ill-considered laws, the English laws against usury were constantly evaded in one way or another. Indeed, evasion was almost a necessity even in the comparatively simple civilization of the Middle Ages. If a man wanted to borrow money he executed a bond—conditioned, let us say, for the payment of 1000 pounds in one year—and delivered it to a moneylender in exchange for the largest amount that he could persuade the lender to advance. If he was so fortunate as to receive 900 pounds, he was thus required to pay interest at the rate of 10 per cent—actually more, since the bond was discounted as a banker would express it, and the interest was, in effect, paid in advance. But the bond might contain, and usually did contain, a penalty clause by which the borrower, in the event of default, became liable to pay 2000 pounds or twice the amount named in the condition. The courts of common law invariably sustained these penalties. Perhaps they did so because, as I have already said, the making of any charge for the use of money was prohibited and if the real nature of the transaction between the parties had been examined no loans of any sort could have been made. However, the taking of interest became legal during the reign of Henry VIII, and when this happened the judges of the common law courts, relying with almost incredible stupidity on the earlier precedents, continued to enforce the penalties. Here the courts of equity intervened. The chancellors declared that iniquitous contracts were void as contrary to natural law, and they granted injunctions restraining moneylenders, even after judgments had been entered in their favor, from collecting more on the judgments than the actual amount of the loans together with interest at the lawful rate.[5] Such injunctions were granted in the reigns of Henry VIII, Elizabeth, and James I, and it seems to me impossible that Shakespeare did not know about them, even though the most famous conflict between law and equity—the one between Lord Coke as chief justice and Lord Ellesmere as chancellor did not take place until after *The Merchant of Venice* had been written.

An American lawyer in commenting on the trial scene has suggested that if Antonio had been well advised he would have caused an injunction to be served on Shylock, thus avoiding the unsatisfactory process by which Portia rescued the merchant from the knife. I have a feeling that the serving of an injunction would not have added anything to the dramatics of the trial scene. Still, I think it noteworthy that no trace of the reasoning of the chancellors creeps into Portia's speech.

[5] The chancellors were more generous than Portia. She refused to give Shylock even his principal.

What she asked Shylock to do was to season justice with mercy. She might have rendered her quibble respectable by declaring that Antonio really needed nothing but justice—not justice of the sort that the "strict court of Venice" had the power to administer, but justice according to a higher and better authenticated law. The English equity lawyers were currently talking sense on this very point, but Shakespeare turned a deaf ear to what they had to say.

The trial scene brings us to the end of the pound of flesh plot. It will enlighten us to listen for a moment to Lorenzo and Jessica as they await Portia's return to her house at Belmont.

Lor. The moon shines bright: in such a night as this,
When the sweet wind did gently kiss the trees
And they did make no noise, in such a night
Troilus methinks mounted the Troyan walls,
And sigh'd his soul toward the Grecian tents,
Where Cressid lay that night.

Jes.   In such a night
Did Thisbe fearfully o'ertrip the dew,
And saw the lion's shadow ere himself,
And ran dismay'd away.

Lor.   In such a night
Stood Dido with a willow in her hand
Upon the wild sea banks, and waft her love
To come again to Carthage.

Jes.   In such a night
Medea gather'd the enchanted herbs
That did renew old Aeson. . . .

Lor. How sweet the moonlight sleeps upon this bank!
Here will we sit, and let the sounds of music

Creep in our ears: soft stillness and the night
Become the touches of sweet harmony.
Sit, Jessica. Look how the floor of heaven
Is thick inlaid with patines of bright gold:
There's not the smallest orb which thou behold'st
But in his motion like an angel sings,
Still quiring to the young-eyed cherubins;
Such harmony is in immortal souls;
But whilst this muddy vesture of decay
Doth grossly close it in, we cannot hear it,

You have just listened to what I suppose is the most beautiful poetic dialogue in any language. Surely it tells us something. We are not in England or, for that matter, in Italy. We are in a nameless country, at once enchanted and enchanting, which has an ethical system all its own and a legal system all its own. According to these systems, if Shylock tricked Antonio then Portia had a corresponding right to trick Shylock. After all, everything turned out very well. We may be sure that Bassanio and Portia, and Lorenzo and Jessica, lived happy ever after. As the editor of the *Variorum* was at pains to point out, Shylock probably had enough left to start life over again with favorable prospects. No doubt he also lived happy ever—well, on second thought, not exactly. No doubt he learned his lesson, lived to a ripe old age, and died, respected by all, leaving a large estate to Lorenzo and Jessica. Let us put the marionettes back in the box, not without a sense of the sadness that inevitably springs from the transiency of beauty.

You will have concluded that I have no very high opinion of Shakespeare's legal attainments and, in particular, that I would not favor the adoption in real life of the legal system prevailing in his enchanted country. It is true enough. Nevertheless, I want to make one point clear—I would rather have written *The Merchant of Venice* than Justinian's *Code* and Blackstone's *Commentaries* rolled into one.

Browning and the Law

IN JUNE of the year 1860 Robert Browning, then happily married to the former Elizabeth Barrett and living with his wife in Florence, Italy, happened upon and purchased in the shop of a secondhand dealer on San Lorenzo Square an old yellow book in crumpled vellum covers. It contained the record of a criminal trial which had taken place in Rome almost at the end of the seventeenth century and which had resulted in the execution of an Italian nobleman and four other persons.

The Old Yellow Book was written in Latin and now belongs to Balliol College, Oxford. On account of the use that Browning made of his purchase it has been translated into English at least twice—once by Charles W. Hodell for Everyman's Library and afterwards, in 1925, by Judge John Marshall Gest of Philadelphia. In his disarming preface Judge Gest notes, without apparent regret, that except for the immense expenditure of time and trouble involved in making his translation he might have learned to play bridge or golf, and adds that, as Browning himself put it,

"the very fiends weave ropes of sand
Rather than taste pure hell in idleness."

When Judge Gest's book was published I was a young man and he was probably about my present age. He was a charming and learned man, and I knew him quite well. The book, which includes a great deal of material in addition to a translation of the original record, has 699 pages and was priced at $7.00—almost exactly a penny a page. Judge Gest once said to me that he doubted whether there were more than seven persons in the world who had read every word of it. I was happy to assure him that my wife was one of them. I can throw no light on the identity of the other six.

Here are the bare bones of the story that Browning found in *The Old Yellow Book*.

Guido Franceschini, an Aretine nobleman of forty-six, was married clandestinely, though with the connivance of the bride's mother, to Pompilia, the thirteen-year-old daughter of a Roman middle-class couple of some means, Pietro and Violante Comparini. The father, who had opposed the match because of his discovery that Guido's representations as to his fortune were false, was confronted with the accomplished fact and agreed to make the best of it. The parents turned over to Guido the dowry that had been agreed upon and went to live with him and Pompilia at Arezzo. Dissensions arose, and after four months Pietro and Violante returned to Rome. Thereupon, on the occasion of a Jubilee year, allowing of unusual leniency in the remission of sins, Violante made public confession that Pompilia was not her own child but had been bought from her real mother, a street woman of the lowest type, and passed off on Pietro as his own. Pietro made this disclosure an excuse for bringing suit against Guido to recover the dowry—as I understand it on the theory that if he had known that Pompilia was somebody else's child he would not have paid out the money. The theory seems a strange one, since Guido was a victim of the deception rather than the author of it, and it is not to be wondered at that Pietro lost his case. He took an appeal, but it was never disposed of.

About four years after the marriage and while the litigation about the money was in progress, Pompilia left her husband's home under cover of darkness and set out for Rome in the company of a young canon, Giuseppe Caponsacchi, in order to rejoin Pietro and Violante. The husband pursued, and on the third morning came up with the couple at the inn of Castelnuovo, one post from Rome. Guido, deterred from violence by his respect for law, as he claimed, or by cowardice, as his enemies asserted, had the fugitives arrested—Caponsacchi in the courtyard of the inn and Pompilia in the bedroom where she lay sleeping. At the ensuing trial Guido produced love letters that he claimed to have found in the possession of the defendants, and offered in evidence depositions of the Franceschini servants as to their frequent former meetings, and the deposition of the driver of the carriage in which they fled as to embraces exchanged in the course of the journey. Caponsacchi and Pompilia denied any misconduct in intention or in fact, denounced the letters as forgeries, and asserted that they had followed the extreme course of flight only as a last expedient to rescue the girl from a course of cruelty to which her husband had subjected her. The court found Caponsacchi guilty but apparently entered no judgment in the case against Pompilia. Caponsacchi was relegated to Civita Vecchia for three years—a sentence so light as to suggest that the judges regarded his behavior as an indiscretion rather than anything worse. Pompilia, though not actually convicted, was nevertheless placed by order of the court in a convent, an institution for penitent women, as a place of safekeeping or custody.

After Guido's return home from the trial, which had been held in Rome, he brought an action against Pompilia for the annulment of his marriage on the ground that her parentage had been misrepresented to him by her foster parents; and she brought an action against him for what would now be known as a divorce from bed and board. The law of Italy did not then permit the granting of an absolute divorce. Pompilia's suit never came to a hearing, but Guido lost his action for annulment on the ground that, granting the alleged misrepresentation, he had not been deceived as to the person of his wife but only as to her antecedents. In a like case our courts would make the same ruling today. The earliest precedents seem to have been less reasonable. According to the law laid down in Genesis, if a man sleeps with a woman believing her to be Rachel, but wakes up in the morning to find that his bedfellow was not Rachel but her sister Leah, he must keep Leah whether he likes her or not. As compensation he can have Rachel too, if he is willing to wait.

Pompilia remained in the convent for only a short time. It was determined that her health suffered from the confinement, and on this account she was allowed to go to the suburban villa of her reputed parents. There, on December 18, 1697, she gave birth to a son.

Upon receipt of this news, Guido with four paid con-
federates set out for Rome, and on the night of January
2, 1698 gained access to the villa by the use of the name
"Caponsacchi," killed Pietro and Violante, and, after
inflicting twenty-two wounds on the hapless Pompilia,
escaped, leaving all for dead. Pompilia's wounds proved
to be mortal, but she lived for four days. The mur-
derers, being unable to get horses, had to travel on foot,
and were overtaken, completely exhausted, on the
following day and placed under arrest.

The trial of Guido and his accomplices began in the
same month in which the homicides were committed.
Both sides were represented by lawyers. Guido was examined twice—once before torture and again after
torture. The subject of torture is a terrible one and I
do not propose to give you any details. I must say in
passing, however, that in the Italy of the seventeenth
century—as also in the older world of Greece and Rome
—there were merciful men who believed, however
mistakenly, that torture was a necessary means for elicit-
ing the truth from witnesses in criminal cases. In the
much more wicked world in which we are living today
it is used chiefly—and with cynical deliberation—to
extort falsehood from witnesses in political cases.

The testimony considered by the court, all of which
was in written form, included the confession of Guido
and the depositions made by Caponsacchi and Pompilia
after their arrest at Castelnuovo. In addition, the dying
declarations of Pompilia were offered and received in
evidence. These had been made to religious persons and
others who were attending her between the time of the
assault and the time of her death, and they would be
as admissible in a murder trial now as they were in the

court before which Guido was tried. When the declarations were made Pompilia was not only dying but knew that she was dying, and under these circumstances the law presumes that the consciousness of approaching death creates a sense of solemnity equivalent to that resulting from the taking of an oath. Therefore the courts relax what is known as the hearsay rule and admit the declarations. I assure you that they can be extremely effective in court, if the witness who undertakes to repeat what the dying person said makes a clear statement.

The issues in the prosecution against Guido were pretty much the same as those that had arisen in the earlier trial. The killing itself was, of course, not in dispute. Guido relied on the defense known as *causa honoris*—I suppose a reporter covering a modern murder trial would call it the defense of the unwritten law—and this in turn raised a question as to the guilt or innocence of Pompilia and Caponsacchi. The court convicted Guido and his four accomplices and sentenced them to death, but since Guido belonged to one of the minor orders of the clergy a stay was granted to permit an application to the Pope for the exercise of clemency. The Pope denied the application promptly, and on February 22, 1698—considerably less than two months after the murders were committed—Guido was beheaded and his four companions were hanged.

On the basis of this sordid story Browning wrote his *magnum opus, The Ring and the Book,* a poem containing twenty-one thousand lines—almost exactly twice as many as Milton required to tell the story of the fall of man. In the course of discussing this poem I hope to impress you with the merits of Browning as a poet and philosopher. Before making the attempt, however, I propose to deal briefly with those characteristics—I think I must say eccentricities—of style and manner that have discouraged and prejudiced so many of his readers.

In the preface to a collection of his poems that was published in 1872 Browning expressed his satisfaction at having lived down the "charges of being willfully obscure, unconscientiously careless, or perversely harsh." He was never careless, and we may be sure that he was never *willfully* obscure or *perversely* harsh. Nevertheless, the truth is that he was sometimes obscure and at other times harsh.

The concluding stanza of a lightly written poem called *Popularity* reads as follows:

> "Hobbs hints blue,-straight he turtle eats:
> Nobbs prints blue,-claret crowns his cup:
> Nokes outdares Stokes in azure feats,-
> Both gorge. Who fished the murex up?
> What porridge had John Keats?"

A critic has said that this stanza "is not subtle, and was not meant to be subtle, but is a perfectly casual piece of sentiment," which will become plain if we once understand that the word "murex" is the name of a sea shell out of which was made the celebrated blue dye of Tyre. The poet himself gave a hint of this to his readers in an earlier stanza of his poem:

> "Who has not heard how Tyrian shells
> Enclosed the blue, that dye of dyes
> Whereof one drop worked miracles,
> And colored like Astarte's eyes
> Raw silk the merchant sells?"

Now that I *have* heard it, and have learned also to identify the murex with the Tyrian shell, the last stanza becomes even bluer than it was, but I am sorry to say that it does not seem to me any plainer than it was.

When *Paracelsus* was published in 1835, John Sterling complained of its "verbosity." Browning was much impressed by this criticism, and beginning with *Sordello* in 1840 he adopted what has been called "the surgical expedient of cutting out the usual connecting words." There is a dearth of relative pronouns, words are jammed together instead of being articulately combined, and there are many sentences that will not parse. Tennyson, who, so far as I know, was not given to making bitter remarks about contemporary poetry and who afterwards became a warm friend of Browning, said of *Sordello* that the first line,

"Who will, may hear Sordello's story told,"

and the last line,

"Who would has heard Sordello's story told,"

were the only two lines in the poem that he understood, and that both of them were lies.

Finally, there is the problem of the bad lines. There is a sense in which this is a special problem in Browning. I doubt whether most of you realize how many bad lines good poets have written. (If you wish to pursue the subject I recommend an amusing little anthology of bad verse called *The Stuffed Owl*.) In most instances, however, the bad lines of any given poet bear so close a resemblance to his good ones as to read like imitations or parodies. Wordsworth, for instance, who wrote more bad lines than any other English poet of the first order, strove all his life to achieve beauty through simplicity. When he failed he achieved only dullness through simplicity. The case of Browning is different—it is hard to believe that the good lines and the bad ones were written by the same person.

Let me remind you of the beautiful passage in *Home-Thoughts from Abroad:*

> "That's the wise thrush; he sings each song twice
>   over,
>   Lest you should think he never could recapture
>   The first fine careless rapture!"

You may search through the literature of the English-speaking peoples from Chaucer to Robert Frost, and you will not find anything more lucid than this. But alas! there is another bird. Not long after the justly famous opening stanza of *Rabbi Ben Ezra* Browning wrote:

> "Irks care the crop full bird? Frets doubt the
>   maw-crammed beast?"

This line will parse and it will also scan after a fashion, but I cannot help thinking of the question that Blake addressed to his tiger burning bright:

> "Did he who made the lamb make thee?"

I feel that I must say to the crop full bird:

> "Did he who made the thrush make *thee*?"

The answer in both cases is that he did.

Let us return to *The Ring and the Book.*

I have told you of Browning's discovery of *The Old Yellow Book.* The ring comes into the title of the poem by way of a figure of speech. If, he says in the prologue, a jeweler mixes pure gold with an alloy in order to make it manageable for the work of hammer and file, shapes and carves the ingot, and then burns out the alloy with acid, he can achieve a ring—pure gold and delicately wrought. In like manner, by fusing a something of his own with the gold of crude, unmanageable fact in the records of *The Old Yellow Book,* Browning proposes to recreate "this old woe," and then, removing with a magic acid-spurt all traces of himself, to leave the absolute truth about the dead and all but forgotten Guido, Caponsacchi and Pompilia. The two translators of *The Old Yellow Book* agree in thinking that the spurt of acid did not accomplish its intended purpose. One of them concludes that the alloy—that is, Browning's personality—corrupted the gold of the original facts, the other that the alloy is more precious than the gold. I am not going to discuss this question. It is unprofitable to press a figure of speech until it loses its shape.

So far as I know nothing like *The Ring and the Book* exists in any literature. What Browning did was to take the Roman murder case and to have each one of nine characters go over the story from his own point of view from beginning to end. In his excellent little book on Browning, Chesterton has called attention to the fable of the five blind men who went to visit an elephant. To the man who seized its trunk the elephant was a kind of serpent; to the one who embraced its leg it was a kind of tree; to the one who leaned against its side it was a wall; to the one who had hold of its tail it was a rope; while the unfortunate visitor who encountered its tusk thought it was a weapon resembling a lance or spear. In like manner Browning's nine characters bring us conflicting reports, not only of what happened but also of motives and purposes—reports which should teach us, he says,

> "This lesson, that our human speech is naught,
> Our human testimony false, our fame
> And human estimation words and wind."

The nine characters are (1) a respectable Roman citizen who fears that his wife is unfaithful to him and who is understandably sympathetic with jealous husbands rather than with rebellious wives and handsome canons; (2) a sentimental bachelor who has been impressed by Pompilia's beauty and believes in her innocence; (3) a cynical gentleman of quality who discusses the crime in a fashionable drawing room before a cardinal, a nobleman, and an ambassador; (4) Guido; (5) Caponsacchi; (6) the dying Pompilia; (7) the attorney appointed by the court to defend Guido; (8) the Advocate of the Fisc or, as we would say, the district attorney; and (9) the Pope, eighty-six years of age, who reviews the records of the trial and decides to deny Guido's appeal for clemency. We listen to Guido twice—once when he addresses the court after having been tortured and a second time on the last night of his life when he knows that all hope is gone and that he is going to be beheaded. Consequently there are ten books, in addition to the prologue (already referred to) and an epilogue. In spite of the presence of all the defects that I have mentioned—difficult allusions, obscurities of style, and bad lines—and in spite also of a good many passages that are undeniably dull, the result is perhaps the most original work of art ever produced.

I should be sorry to be condemned to count the number of times that the word "law" appears in *The Ring and the Book*. Unfortunately this is a word of many meanings. In a book that I once wrote I made a list of fourteen commonly accepted meanings, beginning with the law of gravity and ranging through Gresham's law and the laws of whist to a statute adopted by a legislative body. The list is by no means complete. For present purposes the problem is simplified by the fact that Browning was principally concerned with only two kinds of law—"positive law" and "natural law." A bitter controversy is now going on both in the United States and elsewhere between the supporters of these competing, or supposedly competing, schools. I say "supposedly competing" because I know of no necessary reason why a positivist should reject the doctrine of natural law, although most modern positivists have been philosophic skeptics who have in fact rejected it. Mr. Justice Holmes was a positivist of this sort, and there was a time when he and his followers seemed almost to have won the field. However, since his death positivism has been the subject of continuous attacks from various directions. I am sorry to report that with a few notable exceptions the debate has been carried on with so much acrimony as to conceal or distort the real issues involved. In order to make the matter clear I must do a little explaining.[1]

Positive law is that sort of law with which the science of jurisprudence is concerned—the sort of law that is laid down and established by the votes of legislative

[1] A part of what follows is quoted or paraphrased from my book: *Leviathan and Natural Law*, Princeton, 1951.

bodies, by the decrees of dictators, and by the decisions
of courts. However we may define it, it has a human
origin that can be identified. It is the law *that is,* and
the positivists insist that in order to think clearly and
usefully on legal and political subjects we must dis-
tinguish it sharply from the law *that ought to be*—"wish-
law," as Professor Kelsen calls it. This seems to me an
innocent, not to say obvious, proposition which would
have been in no way offensive to Aquinas, but it arouses
the animosity of the present-day defenders of natural
law. They assert that a rigid separation of the *is* and
the *ought* is undesirable and, in any event, impossible;
and they cite the authority of the Church fathers to the
effect that "a law that is not just seems to be no law
at all," and that edicts repugnant to natural justice are
"void."

In the very narrow issue thus joined I must cast my
vote with the positivists. In the whole history of
civilization—for that matter in the whole history of
barbarism—you will find no more wicked enactments
than those directed by Hitler against the Jews. Nevertheless, they were regularly adopted, they were enforced
by duly constituted agents of Hitler's government, and
in consequence millions of innocent persons were done
to death. If these things were not laws, what were they?
The champions of natural law will answer that they
were perversions of law. As soon as this answer is made,
the issue between the disputants—already narrow, as I
have said—becomes purely verbal. All we need, if we
need anything, is a new word to describe perversions of
law. In my view of the matter, we do not need any such
word. It seems to me both simple and accurate to say
that some laws are good and some bad, though I think

we must add that if a law is bad enough the duty of the citizen or subject is to break it. When the Fugitive Slave Act was passed, the usually serene Emerson wrote in his diary: "I will not obey it, by God." There is nothing in the fundamental creed of positivism to require disagreement with either the form or substance of Emerson's resolution. Bentham, indeed, who was one of the first and most influential of the modern positivists, expressly laid it down that while revolution is never a political right, it may, under certain circumstances, become a moral duty.

So much for positivism. Now for natural law.

I will give you three definitions. (1) Natural law is so much of the law of God as is revealed to men by conscience and reason. (2) It consists of those "principles of conduct [which] are common to and admitted by all men who try to behave reasonably." (3) It is "the expression of right reason, inhering in nature and man, and having ethically a binding force as a rule of civil conduct." You will notice that all three definitions contain some form of the word "reason." You will also notice that natural law, unlike positive law, is not conceived as having a human origin. It has human interpreters, of course, but it comes from some other source.

It is regrettable that so many people think of natural law as a doctrine peculiar to the Catholic Church. This is a misconception. While it is true that most, though not all, Catholics believe in it, the doctrine itself is much older than Christianity and has been accepted by many legal philosophers who were not members of the Catholic Church. Lao-tse taught it to his disciples five hundred years before the Christian era began. The Stoics deduced it from the rational and divine order of the world; and Cicero, who followed the Stoic tradition, accepted it as the basis of his legal philosophy and declared that "the discipline of law is drawn from the innermost nature of man." The English common-law conceptions of a reasonable man and a reasonable price are based upon it. Wherever the doctrine occurs and however it may be expressed, its proponents share the conviction of Aristotle that "there really is, as everyone to some extent divines, a natural justice . . . that is binding on all men"—a conviction that is repeated not only in Justinian's Code, but also in the daily pronouncements of our own equity judges. Clearly, then, if we are dealing with a delusion, the delusion has shown itself to be both deeply seated and recurrent. As Etienne Gilson has said, "The natural law always buries its undertakers."

Nevertheless, there are difficulties here and we must try to reckon with them. Bentham denounced natural law as "nothing but a phrase." I am not willing to admit this, but I am willing to admit that it is sometimes a misleading phrase in political and legal discussions. Guido reminds his judges of "the higher law" of which the law of the land is "humbly representative" and concludes:

> "Justinian's Pandects only made precise
> What simply sparkled in men's eyes before."

This could hardly be said better. Let us concede that it is true so far as Justinian's Pandects are concerned, or at least that it may be true. The fact remains, however, that what causes men to be beheaded or electrocuted, to be imprisoned and released, to be divorced, to pay out money as damages, to keep to the right in driving on public highways, to refrain from trespassing on the land of their neighbors, and to do or omit a thousand other acts is not something that just sparkled in men's eyes. Whether good or bad, just or unjust— whether declaratory of "the felt necessities of the time" or in denial of those necessities—it is something commanded or forbidden by a human agency clothed with the power to enforce the rules that it lays down. Here again, and again on a narrow issue, I must vote with the positivists. Natural law is not "law in the lawyer's sense," but to say this is not necessarily to deny that it may be something more important than law in the lawyer's sense.

There are other and more serious difficulties. It is all very well to talk about "principles of conduct . . . common to and admitted by all men who try to behave reasonably." But can any such principles be discovered? Some men deny it on historical grounds and because they have no confidence in human reason. Pascal, for instance, who was one of the most fervent Catholics who ever lived, pointed out that "we find nothing just or unjust which does not change its character with its climate," and that "larceny, incest, infanticide, parricide, have all had their place among virtuous actions." "No doubt there are natural laws," he said, "but this fine reason, corrupted, has corrupted all."

Other men, preoccupied with what is really the reverse of the same medal, have believed in reason in man but have doubted or disbelieved in reason in the universe. It is apparent that these connected doubts and denials bring us face to face with the most important of all human questions, and it must be equally apparent that I cannot deal with it adequately here. I can do no

more than to express—perhaps no more than to imply—
a personal point of view.

Holmes took delight in describing himself as a
"bettabilitarian"—a word which he coined and which
he defined as "one who thinks you can bet about" the
universe "but not know." This seems to me funda-
mentally sound as a piece of philosophy. My quarrel
with Holmes is that he was such a very cautious bettor.
He wrote: "Speaking only as a bettabilitarian and
within the limits of our very finite experience I have
no faith that reason is the last word of the universe. I
know nothing about it." I know nothing about it either,
and I am persuaded that nobody knows anything about
it. Still, there is a big bet here that I take with alacrity
—not, indeed, that human reason is "the last word of the
universe" but that there is some connection, however
imperfect, between reason in man and reason in the
universe, and hence that truth is more than what
Holmes called it, "the unanimous consent of mankind
to a system of propositions." I think it might even be
argued that this is hardly a gentleman's bet on account
of its heads-I-win-tails-you-lose character. If I win I have
gambled very splendidly. But if I lose I really have nothing to lose, because the world is a madhouse and there
is no sense in thinking at all. I assure you that I am not
attempting a pun when I say that I regard myself as a
better "bettabilitarian" than Holmes.[2]

In *The Ring and the Book* both Guido in addressing
the court and his lawyer in preparing the brief that he

[2] On August 6, 1919 Pollock wrote to Holmes: "For myself I
find it difficult to believe that the universe is reasonable, but
impossible to believe that it is not." This exactly expresses my
own state of mind.

intends to file on Guido's behalf talk at length about natural law, but most of the talk is spurious. Civilizations have certainly existed in which the husband of a woman taken in adultery was permitted, indeed even admonished, to kill her. Perhaps civilizations have existed in which he was permitted to do so more than eight months after the commission of the offense. But I doubt whether there was ever a civilization in which the adultery of a wife was regarded as a justification for killing her father and mother, even if they received her into their family with full knowledge of her guilt. Therefore the plea of *causa honoris,* supposing that it carried some weight so far as the killing of Pompilia was concerned, had no bearing whatever on the murders of Pietro and Violante.

Sometimes, though not always, the Pope speaks for Browning, and it is clear that he does so in determining the objective facts of the case. For the purposes of literary criticism we must accept his conclusion. Pompilia was "perfect in whiteness," Caponsacchi was a chivalrous "warrior-priest," the letters were forged, and the testimony of the servants and others was perjured. It is as simple as that—as simple as the answer of the Delphic oracle to the inquiry about the guilt or innocence of Hermione in *The Winter's Tale.*[3] But is this the absolute truth that Browning promised us at the outset? Not by any means, because there is a significant sense in which Guido is the hero of *The Ring and the Book.*

[3] "Hermione is chaste; Polixenes blameless; Camillo a true subject; Leontes a jealous tyrant; his innocent babe truly begotten; and the king shall live without an heir, if that which is lost be not found."

Chesterton said aptly that Browning "was a kind of cosmic detective who walked into the foulest of thieves' kitchens and accused men publicly of virtue." In *Mr. Sludge, "the Medium,"* in *Bishop Blougram's Apology,* in *Prince Hohenstiel-Schwangau* and elsewhere he concerned himself not so much with what happened in the course of a discreditable career as with the judgment that God has pronounced or is about to pronounce on one of his creatures. When a man stands at the bar of any human tribunal, no matter what kind of law the tribunal purports to administer, the most that he can ask for is perfect impartiality. When he stands at the bar of God we may suppose that he faces a perfect partiality—a complete and loving understanding of every obscure and half-forgotten motive, every frustrated ambition, every confidence betrayed, and every hope blighted. It is this perfect partiality that Browning sought to achieve.

Let us not forget that no sane human being ever joined Milton's Satan in saying: "Evil, be thou my good." When the leader of a criminal gang in one of our big cities shoots and kills his rival in the course of a gang war, he does not admit even to himself that he is a murderer in the sight of God and man. However he may plead in court, he says something in his heart —perhaps that he never had a fair chance in life, and that anyway the murdered man was a rat and deserved what he got. The defaulting bank cashier never tells himself that he is neither more nor less than a thief. He complains that the bank expected him to keep up appearances and that the directors never voted him an adequate salary. To turn from imaginary and trivial cases to a historic case that continues to seem important after nearly two thousand years, it would be interesting, to say the least, to have an accurate account of what went on in the mind of Judas Iscariot during a period of weeks or months immediately preceding the crucifixion. I have no idea what he said to himself, but I do know this—he never said: "This man is the Messiah and I am going to betray him." Instead, he said something else.

Well, what is the case for Guido in the Court of Perfect Partiality? Browning trys to tell us. Guido was not prepossessing physically:

> "A beak-nosed, bushy-bearded, black-haired lord,
> Lean, pallid, low of stature, yet robust . . ."

He was the oldest son of a noble but impoverished family. His two younger brothers went into the Church, but he felt himself debarred from Holy Orders and also from service in the army by reason of his duties as the head of the family. Compelled to provide for himself in some way, he took several minor orders in the Church and, through the influence of his brother Paul, attached himself to a certain cardinal as a gentleman squire. In that capacity he ran errands, waited outside vestibules with messages, kept innumerable fasts and feasts, and

> ". . . rarely missed a place at the table-foot,
> Except when some ambassador or such like,
> Brought his own people . . ."

After thirty years of waiting for preferment that never came, he found himself no longer needed in his patron's household and as poor as when he entered it. An advantageous marriage now seemed the only way in which to retrieve his fortunes. Paul found Pompilia, and Guido agreed to marry her. He never liked her, and she never pretended to feel affection for him. "This wife of mine," he says (and there is a certain merit in the charge)

"Would not begin the lie that ends with truth,
   Nor feign the love that brings real love about."

She was a

"Lily-livered wife with milk for blood"—

a "lamblike wife," who

"could neither bark nor bite,
   She bleated, bleated till for pity pure
   The village roused up, ran with pole and prong
   To the rescue, and behold the wolf's at bay!"

Pietro and Violante were vulgar people of the middle class, and Guido came to detest them. In addition, there was the humiliation resulting from the disclosure of Pompilia's low birth, and the further humiliations of the suit for the recovery of the dowry and the loss of Guido's suit for the annulment of his marriage.

Like most criminals, Guido thinks that he has had bad luck. "Everything goes against me," he says. To be sure, this is not very good poetry, but it has a familiar ring. If he had not happened to encounter "the one scrupulous fellow in all Rome," a bribe would have procured horses to carry him outside the jurisdiction of the Roman court. If Pompilia had not lived "four whole, extravagant, impossible days," he could have told the story that he originally intended—namely, that

Caponsacchi was with her when the murders were
committed but made good his escape.

It is noteworthy that in his final monologue Guido
says nothing about natural law. Instead, he talks about
positive law and the price that a man must be willing
to pay, or at least must be willing to risk paying, if he
determines to break it.

> "I say that, long ago, when things began,
>   All the world made agreement, such and such
>   Were pleasure-giving profit-bearing acts,
>   But henceforth extra-legal, nor to be:
>   You must not kill the man whose death would
>   please
>   And profit you, unless his life stop yours
>   Plainly, and need so be put aside:
>   Get the thing done by public course, by law,
>   Only no private bloodshed as of old . . ."

But Guido was not able to keep the terms of the agree-
ment.

> "I could not, for that foolish life of me,
>   Help risking law's infringement,—I broke bond,
>   And needs must pay price,—wherefore here's my
>   head,
>   Flung with a flourish!"

The law can exact a penalty but it cannot exact repent-
ance, and Guido is not going to repent. He has a low
opinion of the sort of Christianity he has encountered.
If there was such a faith at all, it is "ludicrously dead,"
and all its adherents can do is to boast about

> "What feats the thing did in a crazy land
>   At a fabulous epoch."

If there is a life to come, Guido will reckon with it as
he did with this one.

> "Is there a new rule in another world?
> Be sure I shall resign myself: as here
> I recognized no law I could not see,
> There, what I see, I shall acknowledge too:
> On earth I never took the Pope for God,
> In heaven I shall scarce take God for the Pope."

This is not an engaging picture of a man. Is there
anything else to be said for Guido? Yes, there is.

In *Mr. Sludge, "the Medium"* Browning dealt in
his characteristic fashion with a trickster who posed as
a spiritualistic medium. All of the manifestations that
Mr. Sludge produced were deliberately fraudulent. He
felt nothing but contempt for what he called his "deserv-
ing public," and he realized perfectly that nobody believed in him, or in spiritualism because of him, except
as a result of the frauds that he perpetrated. Nevertheless, he says in his confession:

> "This trade of mine—I don't know, can't be sure
> But there was something in it, tricks and all!"

Perhaps, in short, the tricks induced stupid people to
accept what they ought to have accepted in the first
instance and on other grounds. The case of Guido was
in some respects the same. Although he forged the
letters and suborned the witnesses, he always believed
that Pompilia and Caponsacchi were guilty, or might
have been guilty. It was not Pompilia's flight but the
birth of her child that drove him to adopt the course
of "private bloodshed" that the law had commanded
him to renounce. He cared nothing about his wife but

he would have been proud of a son. When the child was born he did not know whether it was the heir of the house of Franceschini or Caponsacchi's bastard.[4] "Then I rose up like fire," he tells his judges. Much of what Guido says to the court is false or distorted, but this time, like Mr. Sludge, he is speaking the truth.

A final question remains—what was the judgment of the Court of Perfect Partiality? I will let the Pope give you Browning's answer. The Pope is thinking about the consequences in this world and the next of the death sentence that he has decided to let stand. He says:

"I stood at Naples once, a night so dark
  I could have scarce conjectured there was earth
  Anywhere, sky or sea or world at all:
  But the night's black was burst through by a
    blaze—
  Thunder struck blow on blow, earth groaned and
    bore,
  Through her whole length of mountain visible:
  There lay the city thick and plain with spires,
  And, like a ghost disshrouded, white the sea,
  So may the truth be flashed out by one blow,
  And Guido see, one instant, and be saved.
  Else I avert my face, nor follow him
  Into that sad obscure sequestered state

  4 Pompilia left Guido on April 29, 1697 and the child was born on December 18th of the same year, or a little less than eight months afterwards. Under these circumstances the law would have presumed that the child was legitimate. Browning makes this point, although sentimental considerations led him to change the date of the flight from April 29th to April 23rd, St. George's Day.

Where God unmakes but to remake the soul
He else made first in vain."

As rhetoric this is superb. As poetry it is consummate. As theology I am afraid its implications are not quite orthodox. I hope with all my heart and soul that they are true.